BOOK OF

LETTUCE
& GREENS

NATIONAL

Gardening

ASSOCIATION

BOOK OF

LETTUCE & GREENS

Edited by the staff of the
National Gardening magazine

ILLUSTRATIONS BY
ELAYNE SEARS & LYN SEVERANCE

VILLARD BOOKS ■ NEW YORK ■ 1987

All rights reserved under International and Pan-
American Copyright Conventions. Published in
the United States by Villard Books, a division of
Random House, Inc., New York, and
simultaneously in Canada by Random House of
Canada Limited, Toronto. A first edition was
published in 1978 by the National Gardening
Association. Copyright © 1979 by Gardens for
All, Inc. This revised edition was originally
published by the National Gardening Association
in 1985.

Library of Congress Catalogue
Card Number: 86-40343

ISBN 0-394-74991-X

Designed by Joel Avirom

Manufactured in the United States of America
9 8 7 6 5 4 3 2
Revised Edition

CONTENTS

B O O K   O F

LETTUCE
& GREENS

WHAT GREENS NEED

Most greens thrive in cool spring and fall weather (50–60°F). Just compare the crisp, flavorful lettuce leaves harvested in spring with the often bitter leaves of a summer cutting, and, you'll agree. A few greens can handle summer heat, but most of them prefer the cooler temperatures of spring and fall.

A steady flow of moisture and nutrients is important for good greens growth. And for some greens, these supplies have to be near the surface. The roots of lettuce, for example, are close to the surface. They don't grow deep in the soil to search out food and water. If you've gardened in dry times, you know lettuce is not too drought-resistant. Big-leaved plants give off a lot of moisture. When it's dry, they get very thirsty!

Leafy crops need plenty of nitrogen, too. That's the key element in the good growth of leaves and it influences the crispness and quality of leafy crops, too.

A lot of heat is what most greens don't need. Spinach, for example, will quickly develop a seedstalk and start to stretch upward when it gets too warm. This is known as going to seed, or "bolting." When it happens, spinach leaves start to lose some of their flavor. A long hot spell can spoil heads of iceberg-type lettuce, too. The heat loosens the leaves of the head, and they get soft and sometimes bitter. If you can shade some of these crops as hot weather approaches, you can often keep the harvest going pretty well.

But, basically, greens are straightforward to grow—so, let's get started!

THE BIG THREE

"Lettuce

"Lettuce" is synonymous with "salad" for people all over the world. It's by far the world's most popular salad plant and has been cultivated for more than 2,000 years. Ancient records note that lettuce was served at the royal table of Persian kings as early as 550 B.C. And today you rarely see a home garden without some kind of lettuce growing in it.

The uninitiated may think, Lettuce is lettuce. Not so! There is a wonderful diversity of varieties. Each has a distinct flavor, texture, and color, so you can have remarkably different salads just by varying the lettuces you use. Here's a rundown of what you can expect in the lettuce department:

With the price of *head lettuce* in the supermarket these days, it's no wonder that many folks decide to include it in their garden plan. Some people refer to all head lettuce as "crisphead" or "iceberg" lettuce. Crisphead is probably a better catch-all term, since technically *Iceberg* is just one variety of head lettuce. *Great Lakes, Iceberg*, and *Ithaca* are good choices for home gardeners. Those in the South may want to try varieties that are better adapted to hot weather, such as *Premier Great Lakes* and *Montmar*.

Butterhead or *loosehead* lettuce plants form a head, but the leaves don't wrap themselves tightly together. *Dark Green Boston* is a good variety for home gardeners.

It's taste and crispness are terrific. The leaves are crunchier than leaf lettuce. The outer leaves of the head are dark green, and the inner leaves are lighter-colored, sometimes even whitish.

Buttercrunch and *Bibb* are two other good and popular loosehead varieties. You can harvest some loosehead plants before they form heads for an early harvest of tasty leaves. A second crop will follow. To harvest, simply take a knife and cut the entire plant off about 1 inch above the ground.

Leaf lettuce doesn't form a head at all—it grows up and out. It's very easy to plant and will grow anywhere, almost anytime. Make regular plantings every few weeks over the entire season, starting as soon as you can work the soil in the spring. That way you always have lettuce that is young and fresh. Never give the crop time to get old, tough, and bitter—harvest at the peak of freshness and taste. Harvest leaf lettuces by picking off the large outer leaves or cutting the plant off an inch above the ground and letting it grow back.

Black Seeded Simpson is an old favorite and one of the earliest leaf lettuces you can grow. *Oak Leaf* has thin, tender leaves and takes heat well, while *Green Ice* has crinkly leaves and is one of the slowest to go to seed.

Be sure to include some *Ruby Leaf* lettuce, too. It adds great color and taste to a salad, and looks beautiful in the garden.

Cos or *Romaine* lettuce always has a spot in the garden. Plant the seeds very early like other varieties, but plant them a little thicker because Romaine lettuce doesn't germinate as well as other kinds of lettuce.

The plants produce a tall head—10 inches or more—of dark-green leaves that close up firmly. The tight, inner leaves are especially tasty in tossed salads because they often have a pleasant, mild taste. Romaine lettuce takes a little while longer to form a full-grown head—about seventy or eighty days. You can harvest it earlier, of course, just like loosehead lettuce. Cut it before it forms a head, and it will come back to give you an additional harvest.

Paris White Cos is a vigorous, disease-resistant variety with dark-green leaves. *Lobjoit's Green Cos* is one of the earliest romaines, maturing about a week before *Paris White*.

Spinach

Spinach is one of the most versatile greens you can grow. It fits into almost any part of the menu. Delicious raw in salads, it is also tasty steamed, stir-fried with a little garlic and ginger, or chopped and added to soups, quiches, and casseroles.

In addition, spinach is one of the most nutritious greens you can grow. Raw spinach is very high in vitamin A and tasty in salads. Very little of this important vitamin is lost in canning or freezing, so you can pack a lot of nutrition

in your canning jars or freezer cartons. Spinach has lots of vitamin C, calcium, and iron as well.

The leaves of a robust spinach plant are large, and if you've ever grown spinach, you know it doesn't take many leaves to fill a basket. But, when you cook them, they really wilt, and a lot turns to a little.

To get a lot of spinach from a small space, try planting it in wide rows 15 to 20 inches across. Because spinach thrives in cool weather, plant early in the spring and again in late summer or fall for fall or winter harvest, depending on your climate.

Don't be afraid to start your spinach plants early in the season, three to six weeks before the last frost-free day in your area. Spinach seeds germinate well in cool soil, and the young plants grow best at cool temperatures and tolerate light frosts. If you plant too late in the season, you may find that early summer heat and lengthening days cause your plants to bolt—form seedheads—before you have much of a harvest.

Bloomsdale Longstanding is an old favorite of many gardeners. It has crinkled, dark-green leaves and is slow to bolt. *Melody* is a heavy-yielding, disease-resistant variety.

Another good variety is *Winter Bloomsdale*. It's a nice

fall-harvested spinach, and many gardeners, especially those in the South where winters are mild, plant it in the fall to harvest through the cool winter months and early spring.

And then there's *New Zealand spinach*, which is not a spinach at all, but a green that is grown as a warm-weather substitute for spinach. The leaves have a spinach-like flavor and can be eaten raw or cooked, although not everyone finds them very palatable when raw.

The seeds of New Zealand spinach have a hard seed coat. Soaking the seeds overnight before planting will hasten germination, although you can usually get a good stand just from planting in moist soil.

Swiss Chard

Swiss Chard is a favorite green of many gardeners because it will grow well in both cool and warm weather. This ability to grow through the summer sets it apart from most greens, and should put chard at the top of your planting list!

Chard is actually a bottomless beet. It's in the same family as beets, but chard doesn't develop roots like beets. In the large, fleshy stalks and broad, crisp leaves, there are plenty of minerals like the highly nutritious beet tops.

Plant chard in rows about 15 inches wide, scattering the seeds an inch or so apart. After thinning, the plants will be 4 to 5 inches apart. Harvest the first plants when they are about 6 inches high, and cut the entire plant an inch above the ground. In short time the chard leaves come on again. Harvest only a few feet of the row at a time, so by the time you cut your way to the taller plants at the end of the row, the plants you harvested first are about ready to cut back again. This way the wide row of chard will keep producing all the way into fall and early winter.

If you really enjoy chard, make two plantings: one in early spring and another one in mid or late summer. You can plant it in the fall down South.

Swiss chard comes in different colors. Varieties such as *Lucullus* and *Fordhood Giant* are green with white stems. *Rhubarb* and *Ruby Red* chard have bright red stems and reddish-green leaves. All varieties of Swiss chard are good from a nutritional standpoint, being high in vitamin A.

Those chard stalks offer a double delight for the greens grower, by the way. You can cut the stalk and thick midrib out of the leaves and have two entirely different vegetables from the same plant. Just cook up the leaves using your favorite greens recipes and prepare the stems as you would asparagus or braised celery.

GETTING READY

W Planning on Paper

When you think about greens to plant you've got a big group of plants to consider, as well as different varieties of some salad crops. So plan your greens garden on paper when the temperature in the middle of the winter really drops down. It's a nice time to spend an evening or two thumbing through the summery, colorful seed catalogs.

In addition to the "big three"—lettuce, spinach, and chard—why not make room for cabbage-family greens and some lesser-known greens, such as chicory, corn salad, rocket, and escarole? They don't take up much room, and a new green can really spice up a summer salad.

If you're going to plant your lettuce in space-saving wide rows for the first time, you'll have room to try several varieties. Buy an extra seed packet or two of varieties you'd like to try. Planting just 3- to 6-foot rows of three or four kinds of lettuce will give almost any family more than enough lettuce to eat.

If you live in the South, you may want to design your garden to give lettuce and spinach some shade, so they'll last a little longer when the warm temperatures come and push these crops toward bolting.

Planning Tips

Plan in advance to use methods of shading cool-weather greens, or try these planting ideas:

Plant lettuce under pole bean teepees to provide some shade. The bean foliage will shade some of the sun and keep the plants and soil cool. Plant the beans early.

Plant some lettuce or spinach between your corn rows, or on the shady side of a row of tomatoes.

Try multiplanting. Plant lettuce, carrots, and onions within the same wide row (15 or 16 inches across). Harvest the lettuce when young, leaving expansion room for carrots and onions. You can mix and match with other crops, too, including beets and spinach.

Save a window box for a hot green like curlicress. Plant lettuce in a small section of your flower garden, or use it as a decorative, edible border. The foliage is lovely and contrasts beautifully with flowers.

Rich Soil: Greens Love It!

The healthiest and best-tasting greens are those that grow quickly. The important contributors to rapid growth are a steady moisture supply and a fertile soil, one rich with decomposed organic matter or humus.

Make it a point to regularly work plenty of organic matter into the top 6 to 8 inches of soil. Use leaves, compost, grass clippings, garden residues or easy-to-grow cover crops, such as buckwheat, cowpeas, annual rye-grass.

Organic matter in the soil helps it to act like a sponge, retaining moisture. Without organic matter, the soil may drain too quickly, and shallow-rooted crops, like lettuce, will dry out and stop growing. When growth is interrupted like that, food quality goes way down.

When you spade or till all this organic matter into the soil, you are feeding the teeming soil life—those millions of microorganisms that break down the organic matter into nutrient-rich humus. Feed them, and they'll feed you in return.

The microorganisms in the soil and the plants' roots have to breathe, too, and organic matter gives the soil a porous quality so that oxygen can reach the roots.

If you have a heavy soil that doesn't drain well and crusts over after a rain, the particles of organic matter will wedge themselves between the tightly packed soil particles, so that air and water can circulate better.

About pH

Lettuce, spinach, chard, beet and turnip greens, and most of the other greens prefer slightly acid soil—soil with a pH of 6.0 to 6.5. pH is the measure of soil acidity or alkalinity. The pH scale of measurement runs from 1 (very acid) to 14 (very alkaline), with 7 as neutral. (In nature you generally find the range between 4.0 and 8.3.) If your soil pH is too high or too low, your crops may disappoint you. Spinach, for example, will be stunted and less tender when the soil pH is down below 6.0.

To test your soil pH, you can buy an inexpensive testing kit at a garden store or send a soil sample to a commercial lab or to your local cooperative extension service, if they do soil tests. The results may indicate you need to add ground limestone to raise your pH, or you may have to mix sulfur into the soil to lower your pH. Adding sulfur is not common in the East, but adding limestone is. Sulfur is sometimes necessary in the West.

The soil test report will indicate what and how much to add to your soil to bring it into the correct range.

A Scratch in Time Saves

When it's early in the season and nearly time to plant a host of greens, put in a little time with your garden soil to prevent weed problems.

Work the soil once or twice in the week or so before planting time. This puts the soil in good tilth—no clods or soil chunks—and kills early-growing weeds. You see, weed seeds are quite small and must be near the surface where there is moisture and warmth before they can sprout to life.

When they do sprout, you have to look hard to see them. Working the soil—even raking it—will get rid of the tiny weed seedlings before they shoot up.

By periodically going over the soil before planting, you destroy most of the weeds that could be a problem later on. Work the soil one last time just a few minutes before planting. This eliminates most weed seeds that have germinated since your last outing and will give your greens an even chance against the few remaining ones.

Fertilizer

Most gardeners understand that vegetable crops need fertilizer to produce well, but sometimes the questions of what kind, when, and how much can cause some confusion.

The nutrients your leafy greens need are available in commercial fertilizers such as 5-10-10 or 10-10-10, and in organic fertilizers like bonemeal, bloodmeal, and dehydrated manures. By the way, the numbers 5-10-10 or 10-10-10 refer to the percentages of nitrogen (N), phosphorus (P), and potassium (K) in the bag of fertilizer. They're always listed in that order, too: N-P-K.

Nitrogen is essential to all growing vegetation for healthy, dark-green leaves. Phosphorus helps plants grow strong roots, and potassium or potash conditions the whole plant, helping it to bear fruit and resist disease. A balanced diet is important for plants, but remember that we're really looking for quick, steady leaf growth. Nitrogen is the key here. It gives our salad crops their dark-green color and encourages stems and leaves to grow.

Of course, plants need more than just the three major plant nutrients to grow normally. There are secondary plant nutrients, such as magnesium, and some minor elements such as zinc and iron—all important, but usually needed only in small quantities. Most soils have most of these elements, but mixing compost or other organic matter such as composted manure into the soil helps to insure the presence of these minor elements.

The best time to apply a complete chemical fertilizer is shortly before planting time, because you want the nitrogen it contains to be readily available to your young plants.

To apply fertilizer, spread 2 to 3 pounds of 5-10-10 or other complete fertilizer per 100 square feet. (If the fertilizer you use has a higher percentage of nitrogen—in other words, if the first number is greater than 5—use correspondingly less fertilizer. For example, 10-10-10 contains twice as much nitrogen as 5-10-10, so you would use half as much.)

Toss the fertilizer over an area as evenly as possible. You don't want to get a lot of the commercial fertilizer or dried manure in one place. Always mix the fertilizer into the top 2 to 3 inches of soil before planting. Seeds are sensitive and can get burned by any fertilizer that touches them, so spreading it evenly and mixing it into the soil prevents any trouble.

Wide Rows— Greener Garden

What is "wide-row planting?"

Briefly, it involves broadcasting seeds in a wide band, thus creating thicker rows with fewer paths in between.

Not all vegetables, of course, are meant for wide rows. Squashes, tomatoes, cucumbers, and melons are examples of crops that need room to run.

But for greens—including head lettuce, collards, and kale—wide rows offer many advantages. Most important, you can harvest over half again as much from wide rows as from single rows using the same space. With wide rows, it is finally possible to grow lots of spinach in a little space—plenty to eat fresh, plus enough to put by.

Many seasons of wide-row growing and experimenting have shown more benefits than simply greater yields:

Wide rows mean less weeding, because after the closely planted greens grow up to shade the ground, they create a "living mulch" or ground cover that blocks out light from weeds, thus checking their growth. Some hand weeding is still necessary, but the living-mulch in wide rows take care of most weeding.

Living mulch shades the soil, keeping it cool and moist, which is very important for crops like lettuce and spinach that get bitter and bolt when the weather warms up. Wide-row growing extends the harvest into summer because the soil in the row stays cooler. The cooler the soil, the better-flavored crop you'll enjoy.

With summer greens like Swiss chard, the moist soil of a wide row helps maintain continuous growth. There's less drying out of the soil, and consequently, less stop-and-go growth.

Planting is quick and simple. You scatter seed over the wide seedbed with no worry about straight lines or precise spacing.

Wide rows are proven space-savers. You can do away with long single rows of one variety and plant more varieties of your favorite crops. For example, in a 10-foot-long row, 15 inches wide, you can grow three or four kinds of lettuce.

Harvesting is fast because you can reach so many more plants from one spot without moving. It sure beats the nonstop stooping and straightening it takes to harvest or weed single rows.

Time to Plant—Wide Rows

After you've prepared and fertilized your soil on planting day, follow these easy steps to plant your wide rows of greens and salad crops:

Mark the wide row. Stretch a string between two stakes close to the ground for the length of row you want.

Smooth the planting bed. With an iron garden rake, smooth the soil along one side of the string. The rake will mark the width of the row. Don't pack the seedbed down by stepping on it. Always do your work from the side of the row.

Sprinkle the seeds onto the seedbed. Roll seeds off the ends of your fingers with your thumb. Try to scatter them

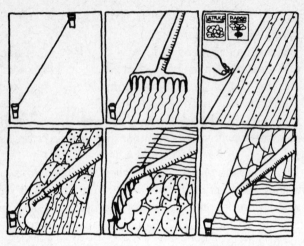

across the seedbed as evenly as you can. The spacing of crops will vary a bit. Lettuce seeds can be planted much thicker than kale or collard seeds, for example. Don't worry if you plant too thickly; thinning will correct that. To give you an idea of how much seed you need, the average packet of lettuce seed will cover about 3 to 6 feet of a row 15 inches wide.

Sprinkle in a few radish seeds. After you've broadcast the main crop, sprinkle some radish seeds down the row. They'll come up quickly and mark the row. Use about 5 percent as much radish seed as the main seed. You can either pull up the radishes while they're small or harvest them after you pick your crop of greens.

Firm the seeds into the soil with a hoe, so the seeds make good contact with the earth.

Cover the seeds with soil from the sides of the row, pulling it up with your rake. The rule of thumb for the amount of soil to cover seeds is two to four times the diameter of the seed. So for most seeds in the green group, that's about ¼ to ½ inch of soil. In midsummer or late-summer plantings, an extra ¼ inch of soil will help keep the seeds from drying out.

Finally, firm the soil once more with the back of a hoe and water gently if the soil is dry.

Single-Row Planting

Use a string to plant a single row, too. Rake the seedbed smooth right over the string, and with the handle end of your rake, make a shallow furrow or planting line along the string.

Sprinkle the seeds in the shallow furrow, and walk by a second time and drop radish seeds every 5 or 6 inches. After firming the seeds into the soil, cover them with ¼ to ½ inch of soil and firm down gently again. Mark the row with the seed packet or a small sign, remove stakes and string, and proceed to the next row to be planted.

Double or Triple Rows

The double-row planting system is just two single rows separated by 4 to 5 inches. It's a garden space-saver, and it is easier to irrigate, which is very important for gardeners in the West and South.

A simple irrigation system can be made simply by placing a soaker hose between the two rows. A soaker hose has many tiny holes in it so water oozes gradually from it, irrigating only the soil around your plants. This is a big water-saving advantage over sprinklers, which also water the walkways.

You can even put three or four single rows 4 to 5 inches from each other and move the soaker hose to each aisle to water all the plants. This arrangement has the space-saving characteristics of wide-row growing and lets you water all the plants evenly, too.

To Win —Thin!

To give your greens the best possible chance for success, thin! Whether you plant in wide, single, double, or multiple rows, you'll need to thin. Because the seeds of most greens are so tiny, we all inevitably plant a little too thickly. That's not bad, though—it helps guarantee a good stand of plants.

You just have to thin out the crowd, so that the plants will have enough room to grow without too much competition from their neighbors. Thinning also provides good air circulation around plants to keep them from staying wet and becoming diseased.

Now, you can spend hours thinning by hand—or you can spend one minute using an iron rake. To thin a row, simply pull the rake across it—with the teeth digging into the soil only about ¼ inch. The teeth remove just enough seedlings, leaving the remaining ones properly spaced. Perhaps they look a little beat up, but don't panic. The plants will snap back quickly and get growing again, better than ever. Rake thinning also gets rid of many small weeds that may have started to germinate, again saving you tedious hand weeding time.

If you want to thin by hand, simply bend over and gently pull up enough plants so the remaining ones are spaced correctly. For example, in the case of leaf lettuce, the plants should stand 3 to 4 inches apart; butterhead lettuce, 4 to 8 inches (6 to 10 inches if you want a bigger head). You can leave 6 to 10 inches between plants if you're thinning collards, kale, or mustard.

Always work the soil just before planting. This clears away any newly germinating weeds and at least puts any remaining weed seeds and your vegetable seeds on an even footing.

Make your first thinning timely. When your vegetable seedlings are about ¼ or ½ inch high, drag an iron rake across the row, keeping the teeth ¼ inch deep. This thins the plants, of course, but it's also your first weeding effort.

Hand-weed as often as necessary until the wide-row greens develop enough foliage to shade out further weed growth.

If you set out lettuce, collards, or other transplants, work the soil before planting them, and wait a week or so for them to take hold before you cultivate near them. In the first few weeks after being transplanted, the plants' roots are quite close to the surface and gaining strength by the day. Don't be careless with a hoe and risk slowing them down or killing them. Keep all cultivation very shallow, ½ to 1 inch deep at most.

Use a good covering on the soil—a "mulch"—to stop weeds around head lettuce plants, collards, or plants in a single row. The hay, straw, or other organic matter will stop most weeds except some stubborn perennials, which will grow through it. Pull those by hand.

Get after weeds when they are small. Don't even wait till they come up out of the ground. After a rain, which will surely cause some weed seeds to germinate, allow the soil to dry slightly and then lightly stir it up with your rake or weeding tool. You kill many weeds before they even appear.

GROWING

W Weeds and Cultivation

eeds are green, and some, like lamb's quarter's and purslane, are eaten as greens, but we really don't want them growing in among our salad crops. They steal moisture, fertilizer, and sunlight. Some of the slower-growing greens can be shaded out of your garden forever by weeds.

There are ways to avoid weed problems in any garden—even if you've suffered from weeding fits in the past:

Try to plant your fine-seeded greens in a section of garden that was relatively weed-free the season before—for example, where your thick, weed-smothering wide rows of beans grew.

Work the soil with a shovel, rake, or tiller a couple of times the week or so before planting. This uproots the tiniest weed seedlings and kills them or buries them (which kills them, too).

Water

You can't beat greens that are crisp and succulent. One of the most important things for highest-quality greens is a steady supply of moisture.

Greens thrive in moist, but not wet, soil. They require about an inch of rain or irrigation water per week, and perhaps a little more for summer greens in hot weather.

If the water supply drops, they may be the first crops in the garden to show signs of drought. That's because many of them—especially lettuce—have limited root systems, and because their large green leaves give off quite a lot of moisture. Sometimes on a hot, sunny afternoon many garden plants appear wilted. That's normal—usually they'll recover by next morning. If they don't, it's time to water.

Here are some tips to help you water wisely:

Irrigate early in the day to cut down on evaporation losses and to make your water go further. This also gives the plants plenty of time to dry out during the day. (Wet foliage overnight allows disease organisms to spread rapidly among the plants.)

Soak the soil thoroughly enough, so that you don't have to come back and water again the following day.

Try to moisten the soil to a depth of 5 or 6 inches, at least.

If the soil is dry at planting time, water as gently as you can after planting, so you don't wash any seeds out. Be sure to keep the seedbed moist until the plants come up.

Solving Lettuce Problems

Let's look at some of the problems you may encounter growing all kinds of lettuce (and some other greens, too).

"My seeds didn't come up." Don't write to the seed company right away. Most often, poor germination is caused by letting the seedbed dry out. It has to be continuously moist. Drying out occurs more often during hot-weather plantings, and not as much with early spring plantings. Sometimes a light mulch of hay or straw to shade the soil after you plant will keep the soil moist until the plants are up. But don't delay in removing the mulch once you see the plants.

Also, be sure to cover the seeds correctly—use just ¼ to ½ inch of moist soil. If your soil gets very crusty and hard before the plants are up, gently run a lawn rake over the surface to break up the hard soil.

"My lettuce is bitter." Bitter lettuce is usually old lettuce, and the older it is, the worse it tastes. Harvest lettuce when it is young—as soon as there's something to eat— and harvest often. Don't wait for leaves to get big. Make frequent plantings of different varieties through the summer, so you'll always have tender sweet lettuce coming in.

"My plants go to seed before I harvest much." Seed-stalks develop with warm weather and long days. It's the natural urge of a plant, and there's nothing you can do

after lettuce bolts.

Bolting won't affect you if you make successive plantings and harvest early. Cut the entire plant off about an inch above the ground. Also, try slow-bolting varieties such as *Oak Leaf*, which can take some heat.

Wide-row planting slows bolting too, as the close-growing plants keep the soil and roots cool.

Diseases

Lettuce is generally a pretty carefree crop. Occasionally some plants, especially those varieties that form heads, will be hit by a fungus disease called *bottom rot*. Rust-colored spots appear on the lower leaves first, eventually spreading until the entire head is rotted. As soon as you notice any infected plants, harvest them, cut away the still usable portions to eat, and destroy the rest. Clean up the garden well at the end of the season to reduce the number of disease-causing spores that overwinter in the soil, and rotate your crops so that lettuce is in the same spot only once every four years, if possible.

Another common ailment of head lettuce is *tip burn*, which causes the edges of many leaves to turn brown and die. It is mostly a hot-weather problem and is not caused by a fungus or insect. Tip burn is usually most severe if there is a lot of fluctuation in soil moisture. Try to keep lettuce plants evenly moist and choose varieties resistant to tip burn, such as *Ithaca* and *Vanguard*.

Be sure to thin your wide rows of greens properly so that the plants have enough air circulation to dry off after a rain or watering. If they're too thick, plants may stay wet too long and develop rot. Continual wetness is an invitation to disease.

Beet and chard greens sometimes develop *leaf spot* trouble. Spots develop on the leaves, usually most severely on the older leaves. Infected leaves may turn yellow and die. Damage is seldom serious enough to warrant any control other than picking off and destroying infected leaves. If your greens are hit with a hard case, applications of an approved fungicide can help to bring the problem under control.

Remember that it's a good idea to rotate the location of the cabbage-family greens (kale, collards, and mustard) in the garden each season to help avoid disease problems.

Insects

Aside from the pests of the cabbage-family greens (see page 41 for more on these), there are few insects that generally cause serious problems. Probably the most troublesome for many gardeners are the small *leaf miners* that feed on spinach, chard, beet, and turnip greens. The immature stage of a small fly, these tiny larvae tunnel in between the layers of leaf tissue, feeding and causing tan-colored blotches on the leaf surface. To control these pests, examine leaves closely for clusters of white eggs on the undersides of leaves, then spray with an approved insecticide three times at weekly intervals. Be sure to observe the recommended time listed on the insecticide label between the last application of spray and harvest. Spraying after the miners are inside the leaves does no good. Another way to control miners is to cover the rows of greens with screen cages to keep the adult flies from laying their eggs on the leaves.

Aphids and *leafhoppers* can be a nuisance in some gardens. These insects can spread certain diseases among the lettuce plants. Aphids are soft-bodied and pear-shaped, and may be green, yellow, or purple. Leafhoppers are light greenish-yellow, small but quite active. Spray with an approved insecticide at ten-day intervals for control of these pests. Keep down weeds in and around the garden, since they can harbor leafhoppers.

The more pungent greens like chicory and curlicress seem to have fewer insect visitors than the milder-flavored ones.

For more information on identifying insects and diseases on your greens, and methods and products to control them, contact your local county extension agent. He or she will be familiar with the ones that are most likely to be troublesome in your area.

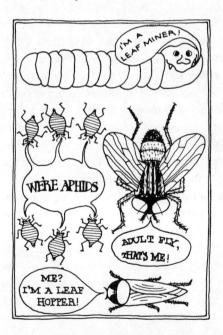

TIPS FOR GROWING HEAD LETTUCE

A lot of people think that crisphead or iceberg-type lettuce is hard to grow. It's not. Good head lettuce just needs fertile soil, ample sunlight, a good supply of moisture and nutrients, and—most important—cool weather. The plants need temperatures of around 55° to 60°F during the growing season, so for most gardeners this means starting plants early indoors or planting in summer or fall for a fall or winter harvest, depending on your climate. Start seedlings indoors in late winter, about six to eight weeks before the average date of the last spring frost.

Plant the seeds in shallow seed boxes or "flats." Put the tiny seedlings in a sunny spot and keep them watered. About six weeks later, the plants are big enough to set in the garden. But before you do that, harden the plants off to get them ready for outdoor living. Place them in a protected spot outside for a few hours a day, lengthening the time they spend outside until they're out there all day.

Our National Gardening Association *Book of Tomatoes* has a lot more general information on starting seeds indoors, caring for seedlings, and how to "harden them off" in case you need some extra advice.

Head lettuce can be started in cold frames if you live where the nights don't get too chilly in early spring.

Gardeners in mild winter areas or where the springs are long and cool can simply sow head lettuce seeds directly in the garden.

Some varieties are noted as "heat-resistant" in the seed catalogs. These are worth trying if hot weather comes too quickly in your area. High temperature over a period of time is nothing but trouble for head lettuce. The heads lose their firmness, the leaves get bitter, and diseases may erupt. So, keep cool—by using mulch, starting seeds indoors, and planning a fall head lettuce crop.

Transplanting Head Lettuce

Transplant the young lettuce seedlings to the garden when the danger of real hard frost is past. They'll take a light freeze if they are hardened off properly.

Putting the plants 10 inches apart from each other in

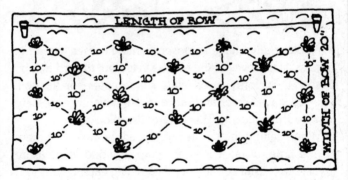

20-inch wide rows is the best way to grow them. Some experts recommend 15 or even 18 inches, but we find advantages in closer planting.

For one thing, you get more heads from a row, and they're better for eating than the larger ones that grow with wider space. Start harvesting heads when they're about the size of a softball—a most edible size. There's no waste and no storing.

You also have a continuous harvest if you start when the heads are small. If you wait until the first head you harvest is the size of a basketball, they'll all be that big on the same day. Start harvesting early, so that you'll have weeks of prime head lettuce. The quality drops off quickly once they reach maturity.

Another advantage to closer planting comes when the large outside leaves of the plants stretch out toward nearby heads. They form an effective shade cover for the soil. The soil stays cooler and more moist, which is necessary for good production. Weeds are also blocked out.

When setting the plants out, dig all the holes for them at one time, using a 10-inch scrap of wood to measure quickly the distance between holes. Dig each hole 4 to 5 inches deep. In the bottom of each hole put a tablespoon of 5-10-10 fertilizer or a small handful of compost or dried manure, and cover it with 2 to 3 inches of soil.

Water the flats well before transferring the seedlings to the garden. That will help keep soil around the roots and protect them from injury. Before you put them in the ground, strip the outer leaves off the plant. Don't touch the center sprout of the plant, though, because that bud will grow to form the head.

Trimming the foliage helps because some of the roots are killed in transplanting, and the smaller root system can't support all the top growth. The roots, which need time to recover, take hold and start to grow again, and find it easier at first to meet the demands of fewer leaves.

Set the plants at the same depth they grew in the flats and give them a gentle watering. Keep them well watered for a few days.

Mulching

A thick, organic mulch (straw, leaves, grass clippings, hay, etc.) is almost a must if you're growing head lettuce down south in the spring. It will help retain moisture and keep the soil cool as warm spring weather arrives. It's good in northern gardens, too, where spring heat or quick-draining soils could hurt the crop.

Cultivation

Cultivation is simply stirring up the soil lightly to kill young weeds and to aerate the soil. Be sure not to kill or hoe around your head lettuce plants deeper than 1 inch— their roots are shallow.

Booster Shot

Head lettuce, like the other kinds of lettuce, has a limited root system that can't go deep in the soil for nutrients. Sometimes an application of extra fertilizer along the way—sidedressing—can help. Make a light application of 5-10-10 fertilizer every three to four weeks. You can also use an organic fertilizer such as manure tea, blood-meal, or cottonseed meal.

 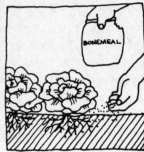

Heading into Fall

Not enough people realize it is easy to have nice fall heads of lettuce, too.

In the Northeast, head lettuce started in mid-July and set out in the garden at the beginning of August will mature in September when it's nice and cool. In warmer parts of the country, it can be planted in the fall for a late fall or winter harvest.

If you are planting a crop for fall or winter harvest when the soil is still warm, lettuce seeds may not germinate well. To overcome this problem (called thermodormancy), soak seeds in cool water for a day, then dry for two hours before planting. Or dampen them and store them in the refrigerator for three to five days before sowing.

To ease the shock of being set out in the garden in midsummer or late-summer heat, shade transplants for a few days and keep them well watered. Spacing is even more important for head lettuce than with other types. Set transplants or thin seedlings 10 to 12 inches apart.

HARVESTING

Harvesting is one of the nicest chores of the gardening season. It's easy to do right:

Start harvesting when there's something to eat. Gardens are for eating, so as soon as your endive, spinach, celery, lettuce, or whatever is big enough to toss in a salad—harvest. There will be plenty more to come.

Harvest at peak flavor and freshness. Young greens are the tastiest and most nutritious. Don't wait for prize-winning heads of lettuce—start picking them when they're softball size, still crisp and flavorful.

If you're freezing or canning spinach, chard, or beet greens, harvest the choicest leaves and plants and process them right away for the best quality.

Harvest lettuce and other greens close to mealtime to retain as much quality and food value as possible.

Try for two, three, or even four cuttings. Leaf lettuce and chard are the best examples of crops that will "come again" after you harvest. If you cut lettuce and chard an inch above the ground, the plants will send out new, fresh

growth in an effort to make seed.

Incidentally, a long serrated bread knife is the best tool for harvesting wide rows of greens.

Easy Cold Frames

A cold frame can extend your green season no matter what part of the country you live in. Cold frames are basically little houses where greens can have a head start in spring and extra growing time in the fall and early winter.

Probably the simplest cold frame is just six bales of hay arranged in a rectangle on the southern side of the house and topped with a storm window. Plant your greens seeds in a flat and place it in the center of the bales underneath the glass.

If you have an old storm window and some planks or scrap lumber, you can put together another easy cold frame. Nail the wood together to fit under the storm window you have. Instead of cutting wood on the slant, just build the frame as a box and simply top it with the storm window. Skip the hinges. On hot days, slide the window to the side to let heat out; on cold nights, put the window squarely over the top of the frame and cover it with an old blanket. In the summer, when you don't need it, it's easy to store.

Cold frames are good for starting seedlings early in the season for later transplanting or for just growing some lettuce, spinach, and radishes, to eat early. In the fall you can grow Boston and other loosehead lettuce and some leaf lettuce for the last homegrown salads in your neighborhood.

THE WORLD OF GREENS

Beets and Turnips: Two for the Price of One

Beets and turnips are special greens because their roots are also edible. Beet greens are most nutritious and taste best when they're harvested young and tender. Fortunately, there's an easy way to have a lot of young greens and still keep plants in the garden for a long time to produce plenty of mature beet roots for later.

The secret is to plant beets in fairly thick, wide rows. Beet seeds resemble tiny scraps of cork—they're bigger than most other salad and green crop seeds. They're easy to space correctly—about an inch apart.

Try about a 15-inch wide row if you haven't planted wide-row-style before.

Plant early in the season, two to four weeks before the last frost-free date. After the seedlings are up, thin with a rake and then sit back and wait for the green bonanza.

Start gathering your greens when the plants are about 6 inches tall. Pull up the entire plant, and if there's a small beet on the bottom, so much the better. Cook it right along with the greens for added flavor.

Detroit Dark Red and *Lutz* are two good varieties. These produce excellent greens and good-sized, tasty beets, too.

A dish of turnip greens may sound like dreary eating —but only if you've never tried them. Cooked with salt pork or bacon, and served with butter or vinegar, greens can be a real taste treat—and very nutritious, too. Turnip greens are high in vitamins A and C, iron, and calcium, and are low in calories.

Turnips are a cool-weather crop, so plant them early in the spring—as soon as the ground can be worked—and again toward the end of summer for a fall crop. Spring is a great time to concentrate on their greens—you don't have to worry about summer heat spoiling any turnips underground. You simply harvest the plants when the roots are small, before hot weather comes.

Fall plantings are popular in the South, too, because in most places you can plant anytime from August to October. The cool fall and mild winter temperatures keep the harvest going for several months. Of course, Southern turnip-lovers plant in the spring, too. In some Southern areas, you can plant every couple of weeks from February to May. With a system like that you'll have nothing but young, tasty greens.

Wide rows, about 15 to 16 inches across, are great for turnips. Plant thickly, and once the plants are 4 to 5 inches tall, start thinning them by hand and boil up the tasty greens. You can eat a lot of greens this way and still afford to let some plants develop big roots below ground.

Some people harvest just the big outside leaves from turnips, so the plants can produce more leaves from the center bud. Others prefer to pull up the whole plant because the small leaves are the most tender.

You can have greens from any turnip variety, but a couple—*Seven Top* and *Shogoin*—are favorites because of their lush, tender foliage.

Cabbage-Family Greens

MUSTARD

Mustard—it's not yellow and you don't spread it on the backside of a ham sandwich. Garden mustard is leafy, curly, green, and very nutritious.

Mustard planted in late summer, about eight weeks before the first fall frost date, is tops for a late harvest. Cold weather and light frosts improve mustard's flavor, just as cold weather does good things for the taste of collards and kale. If you live where the winters are mild, plant mustard in late summer, and you'll harvest greens through the fall and into winter—mustard is quite hardy.

Of course, you can plant mustard early each spring,

too, two to four weeks before the last frost-free date. In as little as thirty days or so, you can be harvesting young leaves, or even the entire plant, if you grow mustard in wide rows. *Green Wave* and *Tendergreen* varieties give excellent results. *Green Wave* is peppery when raw, and *Tendergreen* has a nice mellow-green flavor when cooked

Sow mustard seeds in rich, well-worked, fertilized soil. After the seedlings poke through the soil, thin them with a garden rake. After thinning, the plants should be 4 to 6 inches apart in the row. Start harvesting as soon as there is enough for a meal.

COLLARDS—HEADLESS CABBAGES

The mild cabbagey taste and long tradition of collard greens at mealtime are really special for southern gardeners. Collards are well adapted to the climate in the South; unlike most greens, they'll survive not only the cool spring and fall weather, but also the intense heat of summer.

Some gardeners in the South plant a spring crop, harvesting the lower leaves as they need them early in the season. Then they simply keep the plants growing through the hottest months, and begin harvesting again in the fall. It's much more common, though, to plant collards twice, in early spring and again in late summer.

In the South, collards are so widely grown that garden stores and nurseries provide young collard plants for sale at planting time. Setting out these plants is a convenient and pretty reliable way to have a good harvest before hot weather slows things down.

The 4- to 5-inch seedlings resemble cabbage plants, but they'll never "head up" in the garden like cabbage. Some people even refer to collards as "headless cabbages."

Start collards indoors six to eight weeks before setting them out in the garden, which you can do as early as four weeks before the first frost-free date if plants are properly hardened off.

Collards can also be direct-seeded three to four weeks before the last frost-free date in spring. Fall plantings should go in ten to thirteen weeks before the first fall frost date. Fall collards profit from cool nights and light freezes. That puts the zing and succulence into the leaves.

If you plant collards in wide rows, thin them, so that the plants will be 8 to 10 inches or so apart.

Like other greens, you can start harvesting collards as soon as some of the leaves make enough for a meal. If you harvest only the bottom leaves of the plant, the center bud (where the action is) will keep putting out branches.

Vates and *Georgia Green* are good varieties for the home gardener. The former tolerates cold weather well, while the latter does well in hot weather.

KALE

Kale used to be more popular in our country. Before the days of trucking lettuce thousands of miles to market, local growers provided some of the big eastern city markets with fall, winter, and early spring kale. It helped fill the need for fresh, nutritious greens.

Kale is one of the very best greens if you're shopping for high vitamin and mineral content. It's sometimes called the "Wonder Crop" because its vitamin A and C content is so high. Kale even outranks orange juice in the vitamin C department.

Good taste goes hand in hand with its nutritional excellence. The leaves are tender and sweet-tasting when harvested at the right time, which is after a couple of hard frosts in the fall. The leaves develop a tanginess that is hard to match. Don't stop harvesting if the snows come. The plants stay green and tasty—all you have to do is dig through the snow to get them.

Another peak harvesting period for kale is when the snow melts in the spring and the plants start growing again. The leaves are delicious raw, or you can cook them and use them like spinach.

Kale is not a hard-to-grow or fussy plant. It simply needs well-fertilized, moist soil to get started. But like most cabbage-family greens, after it comes up, you have to make sure it has enough moisture and thin the crop.

Kale doesn't like very hot weather—it's strictly a cool-season green.

For spring crops, plant as early as four to six weeks before the last frost. Plant again about ten weeks before the expected date of the first fall frost for a late harvest. In the South you can plant kale later in the fall and enjoy fresh greens through the mild winter into spring.

A few weeks after planting, thin the plants so they are 6 to 8 inches apart. Later, harvest entire plants to put a little more distance between the remaining plants and really give them room to grow.

Don't worry about mulching kale as winter approaches. While cold weather does kill some of the plants, most survive and put on good growth the following spring. The taste is very good until the plants bolt with warm weather.

Siberian Kale and *Blue Curled Scotch Kale* are the two varieties you'll most likely see in the seed racks. We think the Blue Curled Scotch variety is the better-tasting one.

By the way, the Blue Curled kale makes a nice houseplant in winter. Dig a couple of plants up each fall, pot them, and place them near a south-facing window. The plants lose some color, but the intricate shapes of the curled leaves are quite pleasing.

You might also try planting flowering varieties of kale. Their curly green-and-maroon leaves are beautiful at the edge of the garden—and they also can be potted and brought indoors for the winter.

Cabbage-Family Pests

Mustard, collards, and kale are closely related to the cabbage—and so they suffer from similar pests and diseases.

If you plant any of these greens, you'll have to watch for early-season flea beetles, aphids, and other insects. Spraying with an approved insecticide will control these pests. Be sure to read all directions very carefully before you spray.

The best-known cabbage-family pest is probably the imported cabbageworm—offspring of the white cabbage butterfly. As soon as you see the butterflies making the rounds of your garden, spray every seven to ten days with the biological control *Bacillus thuringiensis*, available in garden stores as Dipel or Thuricide. It's a bacterium that causes the worms to get sick and die after they ingest it. It does not affect the crop or people who eat the crop, only caterpillars.

To guard against diseases that plague the cabbage family of vegetables, be sure to rotate these crops each year. Do not plant them where any other member of the cabbage family—including cabbage, cauliflower, broccoli—grew the previous year.

Endive

Endive is a cool-weather green with a distinct, clean, sharp taste. In recent years it has shown up more often in the produce bins of stores, but it's still expensive.

Endive doesn't like hot weather too well, but it can take some pretty hard frosts. So it's a good winter green down south, where the temperatures are mild. Up north it is grown as a spring or fall crop only.

Plant the seeds directly in the garden, keeping the soil moist until they come up.

For a spring crop, plant seeds in the garden two to four weeks before the last frost-free date. Start fall crops about fifteen weeks before the expected date of the first fall frost. Plant in wide rows and thin later to 6 to 7 inches between plants. You can start endive in flats indoors like head lettuce and transplant it later if you want.

Like other greens, endive tastes best when it grows quickly and steadily. Make sure it gets enough water and fertilizer.

To reduce the bitterness of endive, cut off the light to the heads, or "blanch" them, right out in the garden about a week before harvesting them. Gather up the leaves of the plant and tie them together above the head or cut the tops and bottoms out of milk cartons and slip these homemade blanching tubes over the plants.

There are two types of endive. Curly-leaved types such as *Green Curled* have narrow, frilly leaves. The green known as "escarole" is actually a less curly endive with broader leaves, grown the same way as endive.

Chicory

Chicory grows wild in many parts of the country. It's easy to recognize in fields or along the road when the plants sport many small blue flowers in late summer. Although the leaves of wild chicory are edible when young and tender, there are a number of cultivated chicories that provide the gardener with better eating. Cultivated chicories come in three basic types—leafy types grown for greens, those grown for forcing indoors, and those grown for their roots, which are used as a coffee substitute.

The leafy chicories are a diverse group, more popular in Europe than in this country. Both the beautiful red-leaved varieties such as *Rouge de Verone* and *Radicchio* and the green-leaved, or sugar leaf, varieties that are shaped like Chinese cabbages are sown in midsummer for a fall or early winter harvest. Thin plants to 10 to 12 inches apart. The red chicories are green during the summer, turning red only in the cool weather of fall. Gardeners in the North may find that some varieties of chicory, especially the green-leaved ones, are too tender to take fall frosts, although covering the heads with cloches or hotcaps may be helpful. Leafy chicories have not been widely grown in this country, so there is not a great deal of information on which varieties do best in different parts of the country. There's still lots of room for experimentation with this crop.

Some gardeners like to blanch their chicory for a milder flavor. About three weeks before harvesting, cover the heads with a flowerpot with its drainage hole plugged to exclude light. Do this only in dry weather—wet plants will rot if covered.

Witloof Chicory or Belgian Endive

Roots of forcing, or Witloof types of chicory, can be forced in the fall or in the dead of winter to form nice, tight heads of fresh leaves for salads. Forcing simply means encouraging the roots to use their stored energy to send up fresh top growth.

Sow seeds of forcing chicories in early spring in the North, and in midsummer in warmer parts of the country. Don't harvest the leaves over the summer. You want the plant to put all its energy into developing a large root.

But it's better to harvest the roots, store them, and force them in the cellar in midwinter, when a fresh head of chicory is really a delight.

Dig the roots sometime after the first killing frost. Roots 6 to 8 inches long are best for forcing. Don't brush them

or wash them. Just place them in the sun for an hour or so. Then store them in a cool cellar (40°–50°F) in sand, sawdust, peat moss, or in plastic bags.

When winter sets in, take some chicory roots and trim the root ends so they're pretty much the same length—probably around 6 to 8 inches.

Get a box that's twice the height of the roots and half-fill it with sawdust, sand, peat moss, or very fine soil. Put the roots in standing upright, close together but not touching each other. The crowns of the roots should just be at the top of the packing material. Water thoroughly and then top off the box with another 6 inches or so of more fine sand, peat, or sawdust. Put the box out of the light in a warmer spot (60° is recommended as ideal) and keep the earth moist. Cover the box with plastic or newspaper to keep the moisture in. In three or four weeks you can harvest the tightly folded leaves that sprout up from the center bud of the crown. Cut or snap off the heads at the crown (you'll need to remove the top 6 inches of dry material in order to harvest the heads).

You may have to water again if the lower packing material dries out a bit. Make a hole through the top layer to water. You don't want to wet where the leaves are growing.

The heads are usually just an inch or two in diameter and 5 or 6 inches tall. The leaves are yellowish or white because they haven't received any light. Separate the leaves before serving them.

You can start forcing a box of roots every two weeks or so to have a supply throughout the cold months.

Rocket

Rocket is also called roquette and arugula. The young leaves of this annual green are rough and slender, with a taste all their own—hot, with a hint of bean or nut flavor. Chopped into a salad, rocket leaves can sure keep people guessing about the ingredients!

Cold weather is a must for a good crop of rocket. Sow seeds either early in the spring, or in late summer or fall for a late fall or winter harvest, depending on your climate. Harvest leaves when they are no larger than 6 inches.

Dandelion

Dandelion greens are more popular in Europe than in this country. It's there that several dandelion varieties have been developed to produce larger and curlier leaves.

European gardeners make a habit of blanching the plants to reduce bitterness. If you want to blanch some local dandelions—maybe on your lawn—turn flowerpots over them early in the spring, wait a week, and then harvest the leaves. Just be sure no herbicides have been used on the lawn you're harvesting from.

It's hard to think about planting dandelions as they can be hard to root out if they get firmly established in the garden. But if you're a determined gardening experimenter and want to grow some, plant the seeds in spring as soon as you can work the soil. Thin them to 3 inches apart and later about 5 to 6 inches. Keep picking the green leaves as they reach edible size and as long as they are mild enough to eat.

Corn Salad

This spring and fall green, much prized in Europe, is also called lamb's lettuce, mache, or fetticus. Its leaves have a subtle taste and mix well in a salad with more sharply flavored greens.

One of the nice things about corn salad is its cold-hardiness. It's one of the last crops to quit in the fall and early winter. Start plants indoors in early spring for a late spring crop; in mid to late summer for a fall harvest. In mild climates seeds can be sown in late fall for an early spring harvest.

Sow seeds fairly thickly in a 15-inch wide row simply by broadcasting the seed over the seedbed. Thin so that plants stand several inches apart. You can harvest the young leaves any time after the seedling stage, or you can wait to harvest the entire head in forty-five to sixty days.

Celtuce

Celtuce was introduced to U.S. gardeners more than twenty years ago from China. It was first called "celery lettuce." That's because you can harvest the young leaves of the plants in early spring like leaf lettuce, and then later, as the plants get taller, cut the stems, pick off the leaves, peel the stems, and use them like celery, raw or cooked.

Celtuce is a cool-weather plant for the most part. You should plant it as early as you plant lettuce, but spaced a little farther apart. Harvest the leaves as they reach eating size.

The late spring warm weather will cause the leaves to become bitter, so let them go. When the plant gets a foot or two high, cut the stalk for the "celery" harvest. Trim the leaves off and be sure to peel the stem before eating, raw or cooked.

Curlicress or Peppergrass

This zesty, fast-growing green is low to the ground, frizzy, and adds a curly look to the salad garden. It's often advertised as the plant you can start harvesting in seven to ten days.

Curlicress will grow just about anywhere. Probably the best place for it would be in an indoor flat near the kitchen, where you could snip leaves anytime for garnishing salads or sandwiches.

Chew a few leaves before you decide to use a lot of it in any one dish, though. Curlicress has a fiery taste.

Plant it in short, thick rows early in the year and throw more seeds in every couple of weeks. Harvest early because it will produce little flower stalks in a month or so, and the quality of the sprigs will go down.

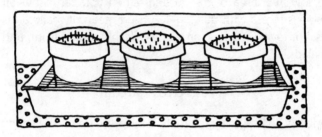

Watercress

Most people think they have to chase around the woods and streams to find watercress. Not so. Though it is more at home in a fast, shallow stream, this snappy, clean-tasting green will grow very well in the garden. You just have to give it a wet spot—preferably some shade, too —to grow in. You'll have to water it often to assure rapid growth.

You can start seeds in small, clay pots set in a pan of water indoors and later transplant them to an outside location when the hard spring frosts are past. Or you can start some plants indoors by sticking some store-bought leafy watercress stems in moist potting soil. Just make sure you keep it well watered.

When the stems have developed roots and are producing new leaves, transplant them to the garden about

6 to 8 inches apart from each other. In four to five weeks, you can start harvesting by cutting off the top 3 to 4 inches of the plants.

Giving the plant the moist conditions it needs will be any gardener's main challenge with watercress. Once you find the right spot—perhaps next to a small pool, or in a low, wet area of the garden—then you can show off your success with this highly prized green. It really adds flavor to sandwiches, omelettes, freshly caught trout, and salads.

Watercress Stream

Here's an easy way to create a false stream on the shady side of the house, so you can grow watercress. Dig a trench (preferably near a downspout or an outside spigot) that will hold a few sections of orangeburg pipe, cut in half lengthwise. (Orangeburg pipe is a manmade fiber pipe—often 6 inches in diameter—used in sewage systems.) You can cut it with a saw. Incidentally, because you're cutting it in half, just buy half the total length you want to end up with.

Butt the sections together and place them in the trench so the rim of the pipe is at ground level. Just about fill the pipe with small stones or stone chips. Then place narrow, perforated plastic seed flats in the pipe trench. Fill them with peat moss and soil, and sow your watercress seeds or put in cuttings.

Let the water from a garden hose or the spigot run into the stones in the pipe sections. As long as the stone bed beneath the flats stays wet, your watercress should flourish—from first thaw to last freeze.

If you have a drainage problem where you've built your stream, you can run a "lateral" of perforated soil drainpipe from one of the ends.

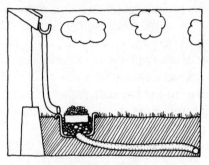

Upland Cress

This cress, sometimes called winter cress or spring cress, is a biennial, which means that it will go to seed the second year of its growth.

Plant seeds early in the spring, and soon after start harvesting the young leaves and sprigs. The plants will survive most winters and send up flower stalks early the next season. You can have a spring harvest of some leaves before the seedstalks appear.

Celery

Celery has a reputation for being a fussy, hard-to-grow vegetable. There's a lot of truth to that, but with the right climate and some care, you can grow large, tender celery. A dozen plants will take up just 5 or 6 feet of row, and it's worth trying.

Celery is challenging to grow because it needs a long

time to grow—up to 130 to 140 days of mostly cool weather—and it's quite demanding when it comes to water and fertilizer. If your soil stays moist and has plenty of organic matter in it, you're in good shape for growing celery. But shut off the water supply even for a short time, and you're in trouble.

The roots of celery plants are limited—usually stretching just 6 to 8 inches away from the plant and only 2 to 3 inches deep, so the top part of the soil not only has to have enough moisture, it must also contain all the nutrients the plants need.

Celery plants don't like hot weather at all—the crop will thrive only where the winters are mild, or where the summers are relatively cool, or where there's a long, cool growing period in the fall.

Because celery takes such a long time to grow, in most parts of the country it's best to start the seeds in plant boxes or flats indoors to get a jump on the season.

Celery seeds are slow to germinate, so soak them overnight to speed up the process. Plant them indoors ten to twelve weeks before the last frost.

When the plants are 2 inches high, transplant them to individual peat pots or to another, deeper flat with new potting soil. If you use flats, put the plants at least 2 inches apart.

Transplant celery to the garden as early as a week or two before the last frost date. Plants should be about 4 to 6 inches high when you set them out. Be sure to harden off plants first, for a week to ten days, to get them used to spring weather. If the weather turns cold after you set your celery out (night temperatures consistently under 55°F for about two weeks), the plants may go to seed prematurely. But because of the need for a long growing season, it's often worth the gamble to set at least some plants out early.

To transplant celery, first work the soil, mixing in the fertilizer (about 1 pound of 5-10-10 per 30 square feet). Remove some of the outside leaves from each plant before setting them in. As with head lettuce, this trimming helps the roots recover from the transplant shock and resume normal growth more quickly.

Space the plants about 8 inches apart, setting them a little deeper than they were growing in the flat. Mulch the plants after they are about 6 inches tall to help keep the soil moist and roots cool. It will also help to keep down weeds, which is important because celery grows slowly and doesn't appreciate any competition from weeds. If you don't mulch, be careful not to weed too deeply near plants. Celery has a shallow root system that can be harmed by deep cultivation.

Sidedressings of 5-10-10 or similar balanced fertilizer in the second and third month of growth will help keep celery growing steadily. Use 1 Tablespoon per plant, and sprinkle it in a shallow furrow about 3 to 4 inches from the plant and cover it with soil.

Give your plants plenty of water. If celery is short on moisture, or a hot spell hits, the stalks get tough and stringy. They can also develop hollow or pithy stalks in dry spells.

When celery gets big enough to eat, start harvesting the larger, outer stalks as you need them. The center will keep producing stalks. To harvest big plants at the end of the season, simply pull up the whole plant and trim off the roots.

Blanching

Unblanched celery has a deeper green color and a stronger flavor than blanched celery, and it is higher in nutrition. If you prefer the taste of blanched celery, try some of the self-blanching varieties such as *Golden Self-Blanching*.

Or you can open the tops and bottoms of half-gallon milk cartons and use these "sleeves" to blanch your celery. Set the cartons over the plants a week, ten days, or even longer before you want to harvest. The color of the stalks will lighten, and their flavor will become milder.

Some people place boards close along each side of the row to blanch celery. Others simply bring soil or mulch up around the plant to block out the sun, although this method may let dirt fall into the interior of the stalks, making them hard to clean. Plants should be dry if blanched with soil or else they may rot.

There's no need to blanch the top leaves, of course, just the stalks.

Storing

Celery stores really well—you can keep it for many weeks with no trouble. Dig up the plants carefully, disturbing the roots as little as possible. Replant them in boxes of sand in your root cellar or set them close together in a trench in your cold frame, where you can keep them from freezing. As long as the roots stay moist and the stalks dry, they'll really keep. Temperatures in the range of 35 to 40°F are best for storage.

FAVORITE RECIPES

Salads

Good salads are easy to make and they are wonderful to eat. Unfortunately, bad salads are also easy to make. Two important rules for excellent salads are:

1. use the freshest, cleanest greens available and
2. use a delicious, homemade dressing.

Fortunately, a tasty salad dressing is easy to make. Basic oil and vinegar dressing—vinaigrette—takes less than two minutes from start to finish. If you want to dress it up a bit, it may take a moment longer.

Good-quality ingredients are important for the best flavor. Although any type of vegetable oil can be used, many prefer the special flavor of olive oil. A mild vinegar —perhaps a wine or herb vinegar—gives just enough flavor without overpowering the flavor of the entire dressing. No matter how much dressing you make, the proportion of oil to vinegar remains the same: 3 to 1.

BASIC VINAIGRETTE DRESSING

3 Tbsp olive oil or other vegetable oil
1 Tbsp vinegar
¼ tsp dry mustard
   salt and freshly ground pepper, to taste

Combine all the ingredients in a jar or bowl and shake or mix until well blended. (Dry mustard may not be used by purists, but it gives the dressing a sparkle that many people enjoy.)

Various seasonings and extras can be added. Fresh or dried herbs such as dill or basil are good. Crumbled bleu cheese or chopped green pepper or chopped onion are other possibilities.

Dress the salad just before serving, tossing well so that the greens are evenly and lightly coated with dressing.

One way to wreck a salad is to use too much dressing. It can drown the salad and make the greens limp and soggy. If you find there's a lot of dressing left in the bowl after the salad is gone, you're using too much dressing —hold back a little next time.

Greens Preparation

Washing lettuce is very important, because greens are magnets for dirt. Nothing ruins a salad faster than having grit as the surprise ingredient.

Because oil and water don't mix, lettuce leaves also need to be dried before being mixed with salad dressing. If they are not dry, they won't accept a coating of oil, and the dressing will just end up in the bottom of the bowl.

Wash leafy greens in several changes of water, letting the grit settle to the bottom and lifting out the greens while changing the water. Be careful not to bruise the leaves.

To dry leaf lettuce, wrap the leaves lightly in a clean towel and pat dry. You can also drain them in a colander or swing them in a wire salad basket. Many people swear by salad spinners for drying and storing lettuce.

To wash head lettuce, core the solid part of the stem and hold the head upside down under running water. Place on a terry towel in the refrigerator and cover with another towel. In a few hours the lettuce will be dry.

If you need to store lettuce, wash it first, wrap it in a damp towel, and store it in a plastic bag or tightly covered container in the refrigerator.

BASIC BLENDER MAYONNAISE

*H*omemade mayonnaise really does taste quite different and much better than store-bought. It's not hard to make if you have a blender.

1 egg yolk
½ tsp dry mustard
½ tsp salt (optional)
   dash of cayenne pepper
2 Tbsp lemon juice
1 cup salad oil, olive oil, or mixture

Put egg yolk, mustard, salt, and cayenne in blender and blend for thirty seconds at high speed. Add lemon juice and blend an additional ten seconds. While blending at high speed, very gradually add oil—in droplets, especially at first. Use rubber spatula if necessary to keep

ingredients flowing to processing blades.

All of a sudden in the blending process, the sound of the blender will change as the mayonnaise thickens, and then you know it's almost done. Go very gently at this point in adding additional oil. Mayonnaise is an emulsion or suspension of egg in oil, and the oil can only hold so much before the whole thing separates. If it does separate, don't despair. Simply remove the mixture from the blender and start with another egg. After it is beaten thoroughly, gradually add the mixture to it and perhaps just a little more oil until it has reached the right consistency.

For a different taste, add one or a combination of the following to the mayonnaise base:

Almonds,
  chopped
Anchovies
Basil
Catsup
Capers
Chervil
Chili powder
Chili sauce
Chives
Curry powder
Dandelion
  greens
Dill

Dry sherry
Egg, hard-
  cooked
Fennel
Garlic, minced
Green pepper
Horseradish
Nasturtium
  leaves
Olives
Onion, grated
Paprika
Parsley
Pickles

Pimiento
Sour cream
Spinach
  leaves,
  chopped
Tabasco sauce
Tarragon
Tomato,
  chopped
Watercress
Whipping
  cream
Yogurt

CREAMY SALAD DRESSING

1 tsp egg yolk
½ tsp dry mustard
  dash of Tabasco sauce
½ tsp minced garlic
  salt and freshly ground pepper to taste
1 tsp vinegar
½ cup olive oil (or peanut, vegetable, or corn oil)
1 to 2 tsp lemon juice (fresh, preferably)
1 tsp heavy cream

Beat an egg yolk and put 1 tsp of it in a mixing bowl. Add the mustard, Tabasco sauce, garlic, salt, pepper, and vinegar. To blend the ingredients well, beat with a wire whisk. Gradually add the oil, beating vigorously until dressing is thickened and well blended. Add the lemon juice and beat in the heavy cream. Makes about ¾ cup, sufficient for 10 to 12 cups of salad greens.

HOT BACON DRESSING

¼ lb bacon
½ cup diced onion
¼ cup white vinegar
¼ cup red wine vinegar
¼ tsp salt (optional)
    pinch of pepper
¼ tsp sugar
1½ tsp cornstarch
½ cup beef broth

   Sauté bacon in large pan until crisp. Drain and set aside.

   Sauté onion in bacon drippings until soft. Stir in vinegars, salt, pepper, and sugar.

   Blend cornstarch and 2 Tbsp of beef broth in a small cup. Add remaining broth to pan and stir in cornstarch mixture.

   Cook over low heat, stirring constantly until thick. Pour over salad greens and toss. Sprinkle with crumbled bacon and serve.

CREAMY THOUSAND ISLAND DRESSING

½ cup mayonnaise
½ cup chili sauce
1 tsp Worcestershire sauce
2 or 3 drops Tabasco sauce
½ tsp salt (optional)
¼ tsp paprika
2 Tbsp chopped celery
2 Tbsp pickle relish
2 Tbsp stuffed olives, chopped
1 tsp minced onion
1 hard-cooked egg, chopped
½ cup sour cream

Combine mayonnaise, chili sauce, Worcestershire, Tabasco, salt, and paprika in a bowl. Mix in remaining ingredients except for sour cream. Fold in sour cream. Chill well. Will keep in the refrigerator for up to one month. Makes 1 pint.

TANGY RUSSIAN DRESSING

    2 cups mayonnaise
 1½ cups chili sauce
   ⅓ cup minced celery
   ⅓ cup minced dill pickle
    2 Tbsp lemon juice
    1 Tbsp Worcestershire sauce
    1 tsp horseradish sauce

Mix all ingredients well and chill. Traditionally served on wedges of head lettuce, especially iceberg. It is also excellent on Swiss cheese and roast beef sandwiches.

HONEY DRESSING

   ⅓ cup honey
    1 cup wine vinegar
    1 clove garlic, finely chopped
    1 cup salad oil

Mix or shake all ingredients in a tightly covered jar and chill. Excellent on spinach greens.

66 SUPER SALAD ADDITIONS

Fresh greens don't require a lot of extras because they are so good plain. They can just be combined with each other—different textures, colors, and flavors—and taste wonderful. There are traditionalists who shudder at the thought of sullying their salads with anything not green, but an occasional addition can really perk up a salad. So here, in alphabetical order, is a list of everything we could think of that can be added to a salad. Some are good in combination; some are good alone. How much you use depends on your mood, the rest of the meal, and what you happen to have on hand.

Anchovies
Apple chunks
Avocado
Bacon
Basil
Bean sprouts
Beets and
   beet greens
Bermuda
   onion slices
Bleu cheese
Capers
Carrots
Carrot curls
Cauliflowerets
Celery
Chervil
Chicken bits
Chives
Cottage cheese
Crabmeat
Cress
Croutons
Cucumber
   slices
Curry powder

Dill
Feta cheese
Eggs
Garlic
Grapes—
   green or
   purple
Green onions
Ham
Horseradish
Kidney beans
Leeks
Lobster
Marjoram
Mayonnaise
Mint
Mushrooms
Nasturtium
   leaves,
   flowers
Nut meats
Olives—ripe
   or green
Parmesean
   cheese
Parsley

Pearl onions
Peppers—
   green or red
Pickles
Pimiento
Pine nuts
Radishes
Roquefort
   cheese
Salami
Salmon
Sardines
Shallots
Shrimp
Snap beans
Snow pea pods
Spinach
Sunflower
   seeds
Swiss chard
Swiss cheese
Tarragon
Tomatoes
Tongue
Tuna fish
Turkey bits

VEGETABLES À LA GRECQUE

Certain vegetables simmered in an aromatic broth and then chilled are wonderful and special accompaniments to a salad, especially if you serve the salad as the first course.

The following vegetables are best suited for à la Grecque preparation. Use them separately or combine a few.

Artichoke hearts	Celery hearts or stalks	Pearl onions
Asparagus	Green beans	Peeled eggplant fingers
Carrots	Leeks	Whole green onions
Cauliflowerets	Mushrooms	Zucchini slices

The broth for 4 cups of vegetables:

2 cups water
¼ cup olive oil
1 garlic clove, crushed
½ tsp salt (optional)
⅓ cup lemon juice
2 Tbsp minced green onion or shallots
¼ cup dry white wine
2 Tbsp chopped parsley
1 small celery stalk
 pinches of thyme, tarragon
1 bay leaf
6 black peppercorns

Simmer all ingredients for ten minutes in a covered saucepan. Add selected vegetables and simmer until barely tender. Do not overcook! Because various vegetables have different cooking times, add the longest-cooking first. Set the timer, and add shorter-cooking ones later to have them all finish together.

Remove vegetables with slotted spoon and put in separate bowl. Boil down broth until there is only about ⅓ cup. Strain it over vegetables and allow to cool. If refrigerated, the vegetables will keep for a few days, but they may be served in a salad as soon as they have cooled.

Spinach

Spinach is delicious, but only if it's been cooked right. Overcooked, it's mushy, slimy, and bitterly metallic. Cooked gently, it has a distinct flavor that is wonderful as an accompaniment to fish, eggs, chicken, roasts; as a separate course in quiche or soufflé; or raw, as a salad. One pound of fresh spinach cooks down to about 1 cup, and that is almost enough for two people.

Spinach, like other greens, must be washed well. To serve it plain, just leave the water of the last washing on the leaves, and put the spinach in a large enamel, Pyrex, or stainless steel pot.

Or use a steamer that has an inner container full of holes that sits over, not in, about 2 inches of boiling water in the outer container. Cover and cook over low to medium heat. In a few minutes, the spinach will be tender, tasty, and ready to serve. Some people like to add vinegar or a sprinkling of nutmeg.

Precooked, chopped spinach is tasty baked in cream sauce, cheese sauce, or with grated Swiss cheese and topped with bread crumbs.

EASY CREAM OF SPINACH SOUP

¼ cup chopped onion
¼ cup margarine or butter
3 Tbsp flour
   salt and pepper to taste
3 cups milk
1 lb (3 cups) chopped spinach or chard

Sauté onion in margarine or butter in heavy saucepan until translucent. Stir in flour, salt, and pepper. Add milk gradually, stirring constantly. Cook over low heat to boiling. Simmer and stir for one minute.

Steam well-washed, chopped spinach or chard until it is just tender. Add to cream sauce base and serve.

SPINACH RING

3 Tbsp finely chopped onion
2 Tbsp margarine or butter
2 cans cream of mushroom soup
3 cups chopped spinach or chard, cooked
½ cup bread crumbs
   salt and pepper to taste
   nutmeg to taste
2 eggs, separated

Preheat oven to 375°. Sauté onion in margarine or butter until tender. Heat the soup, undiluted, stirring until smooth. Add the onions and margarine, spinach, bread crumbs, salt, pepper, and nutmeg.

Beat egg yolks until thick. Stir the egg yolks into spinach mixture, very slowly. Set aside. Beat egg white until stiff but not dry. Fold into spinach mixture and pour into buttered ring mold. Set the mold in a pan of hot water and bake forty-five minutes or until set. Unmold and serve hot. Very good with baked or roast chicken. Serves 6.

POPEYE BURGERS

2 lbs raw spinach, chopped
2 lbs ground beef
½ cup bread crumbs
½ cup shredded Cheddar cheese
2 Tbsp Worcestershire sauce
1 egg, slightly beaten
1 garlic clove, finely minced
   salt and pepper to taste
2 Tbsp oil or margarine

Mix all ingredients well. Shape into 8 patties and cook in oil in large frying pan over medium heat until desired doneness. Turn only once. The patties may also be broiled. May be served on bread or hard rolls, or just plain with mashed potatoes. Serves 4.

LAMB AND SPINACH STEW

    2 lbs boneless lamb stew meat, cubed
    2 Tbsp flour
    2 medium onions, chopped
 1½ cups stock or bouillon
    1 bay leaf
    3 lbs fresh spinach, well washed and chopped
    3 cups diced tomatoes
    1 tsp salt (optional)
  ½ tsp dried rosemary
  ½ tsp freshly ground black pepper
    2 Tbsp flour
    2 Tbsp butter

   Dredge cubed stew meat in flour and brown in Dutch oven. Drain fat, leaving only about 1 Tbsp. Add onions and cook until they are translucent. Add stock and bay leaf and simmer, covered, until tender, about one hour. Add spinach, tomatoes, salt, rosemary, and pepper and cook for about ten minutes, or until spinach is wilted. Blend additional flour with butter and add gradually to stew to thicken. Stir constantly and cook for an additional minute. Serve with rice. Serves 6.

SPINACH/NOODLE CASSEROLE

  1 pound noodles
1½ lbs fresh spinach, well washed
  1 Tbsp lemon juice
  1 Tbsp finely chopped onion
  1 garlic clove, finely minced
  3 Tbsp butter
  3 Tbsp flour
  1 cup light cream or milk
    salt and pepper to taste
    pinch of nutmeg
  ½ cup finely chopped ham
  ½ cup buttered soft fresh bread crumbs

Preheat oven to 350°. Cook noodles until just tender and drain. Lightly steam spinach and chop finely. Add lemon juice. Sauté onion and garlic in butter. Add flour and gradually stir in cream or milk over gentle heat. Season with salt, pepper, and nutmeg. Add spinach and stir well. Add noodles and ham and place in shallow, buttered baking dish. Top with crumbs and bake for twenty minutes, or until lightly browned.

Celery

We've heard that you burn more calories eating raw celery than you consume. That may be the reason celery is on almost every diet invented. But it also tastes good and has an appealing texture that helps you to think you are eating something far more substantial. Celery has a wonderful flavor for soups, stews, and salads that makes it an indispensable vegetable.

To prepare raw celery, wash it well, cut it into uniform strips, and eat it plain or serve it with a dip. It can also be filled with a mixture of bleu cheese and heavy cream.

To keep celery crisp, simply stick the stalks in ice water in the refrigerator, and they'll stay for days.

To boil celery, slice washed stalks crosswise into 1-inch slices. Boil it gently in salted water until crispy-tender. It can be served plain with butter or in cream sauce or Hollandaise.

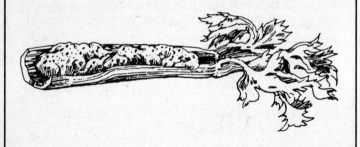

BRAISED CELERY

Wash enough stalks to make four per person, served. If they are large, cut in half. Place in a lidded sauté pan and sauté in clarified butter for two minutes. Add salt and pepper and barely cover with hot chicken or veal stock. Cover and simmer until tender; remove the stalks to individual serving plates and keep warm in oven. Reduce the stock by at least half. Add again as much heavy cream and bring to a boil, stirring constantly. Add ¼ to ½ cup shredded mild cheese and stir until thickened. Pour some sauce over each serving, and top with an "X" of pimiento.

CURRIED CELERY

Cut one whole (large) bunch, or two small ones, into bite-sized pieces crossways. Pare, core, and dice 1 large apple; peel and dice 1 medium onion. Melt chicken fat or lard (or substitute oil and butter) to the point of fragrance, and add the vegetables. Cook and stir until just barely beginning to brown. Turn down the heat and add 1 cup of stock (or bouillon) mixed with 1 Tbsp cornstarch, 1 tsp (or more) curry powder, 2 tsp capers, a pinch of ground ginger, and salt and pepper. Cook over low heat, stirring regularly, until thickened and tender.

GREENS ONE-DISH SUPPER

All greens are delicious cooked with salt pork.

4 lbs greens (beets, chard, spinach, turnip, mustard)
½ lb salt pork
8 small potatoes

Slice salt pork down to the rind. Cover and simmer in sufficient water for one and a half hours. Wash greens in several changes of water. Add potatoes and well-washed greens to salt pork, and more water if necessary, and cook until potatoes are tender—about thirty additional minutes. Drain. Serves 4 to 6.

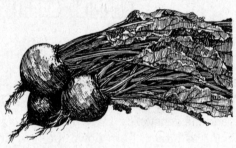

COLLARDS AND MASHED POTATOES

Cook the collards and potatoes in separate pans with water. Drain both. Chop the collards finely and mix with the mashed potatoes. Put in a baking dish in a 400° oven, dot with butter, and bake until browned.

CORNMEAL DUMPLINGS

An excellent accompaniment for the one-dish supper!

- **1 cup flour**
- **½ tsp salt (optional)**
- **2 tsp baking powder**
- **1 cup cornmeal**
- **1 beaten egg**
- **⅔ cup milk**

Sift flour, salt, baking powder. Add cornmeal and beaten egg and milk. Stir well, but do not beat smooth. Drop the dumplings on top of the boiling greens and potatoes by spoonfuls. Cover and cook 15 minutes.

EGG SAUCE

A nice accompaniment for hot cooked greens, especially beet greens, spinach, chard, and kale.

- **1 hard-boiled egg, chopped**
- **¼ tsp salt (optional)**
- **2 slices bacon, cooked and crumbled**
- **2 Tbsp mayonnaise**
- **½ tsp grated onion**

Mix all ingredients together and serve on hot greens.

SIMPLE WATERCRESS SOUP

    1 lb peeled, diced potatoes
    1 lb peeled, sliced onion
 1½ quarts water or chicken stock or broth
    1 Tbsp salt
  ¼ lb watercress
       salt and pepper to taste
    2 Tbsp butter
    2 Tbsp whipping cream
    2 Tbsp chopped parsley or chives

Simmer the potatoes and onion together in water or stock with salt until tender. Liquefy in blender or food processor. Chop watercress finely and add to soup. Simmer for 5 minutes. Add salt and pepper. Remove from heat and add butter and cream and serve. Decorate with chopped parsley or chives. May be served hot or cold. Serves 6 to 8.

ENDIVE QUICHE

Quiche is nothing more, really, then scrambled egg pie with extras thrown in, but it tastes special.

- **4** cups chopped Belgian endive, raw (or cooked spinach, chard, or other greens)
- **¼** tsp salt (optional)
- **2** Tbsp water
- **1** tsp lemon juice
- **2** Tbsp butter or margarine
- **3** eggs
- **1½** cups whipping cream
  pinch of mace
  freshly ground black pepper
- **8″** partially baked pie shell
- **¼** cup grated Swiss cheese
- **1** Tbsp butter or margarine

Preheat oven to 325°. Place endive in 2-quart, buttered baking dish. Mix salt, water, and lemon juice together and pour over endive. Cut a piece of brown paper the same size as the top of the baking dish, butter it, and place it on top of the endive. Cover the dish and braise the endive in the oven for twenty to thirty minutes, or until tender.

While the endive is cooking, beat eggs until thick and beat in cream, mace, and pepper. Remove endive from oven and drain. Turn oven up to 375°.

Fold endive into egg mixture, pour into pastry shell, and sprinkle with cheese and dot with butter.

Bake in upper part of oven for twenty-five to thirty minutes, or until set. Serves 4 to 6.

STIR-FRIED KALE

8 cups fresh kale
4 Tbsp vegetable oil
  salt and pepper to taste

Wash kale leaves and drain.

Heat heavy skillet, electric frying pan, or wok and add oil. When the oil is almost smoking, put in the kale. Toss and stir until it is wilted completely. Stir and cook another five minutes. Great served with chicken fricassee. Serves 4.

WILTED LETTUCE

2 medium heads Boston lettuce *or*
1 medium head Cos *or* equivalent leaf lettuce
6 slices bacon
⅓ cup mild vinegar
  salt and pepper to taste

Wash lettuce well and tear into bite-size bits. Fry bacon until crisp. Remove bacon from pan and crumble. To fat in frying pan, add vinegar, salt, and pepper. When the mixture boils, add the greens and stir until they are just wilted. Serve hot with bacon crumbles on top. Serves 4.

Dandelion Greens

Most people who eat dandelion greens don't plant them. They just pick them wild early in the spring in meadows and pastures—or on their own lawns. Just make sure no herbicides have been used on the lawn you're picking from.

Well-washed, young dandelion greens are very tasty served raw with sour cream.

If you want to serve cooked dandelion greens, wash them well in several changes of water. Put them in a large pot and cover with boiling water, then simmer for five minutes. Drain and add fresh boiling water to them and cook until tender. Drain again and serve hot with butter or margarine or vinegar and salt and pepper to taste. If you like a more tangy flavor, cook them in just one water until tender.

CANNING GREENS

To can greens safely, they must be cooked a long time. Unfortunately, most greens taste their best when very lightly cooked. So while canning is no substitute for fresh greens, canned greens do work well in soups and casseroles.

1. For safety and health, it is important to be careful canning, and the first requirement is to use a pressure canner with an accurate gauge for canning all greens.

For complete instructions and precautions for pressure canning, please carefully read and follow the instruction booklets that accompany your canner and your jars.

For basic canning information contact your local co-operative extension office. They usually have free or low-cost publications with the latest information on safe food preservation techniques. You can also write for USDA Bulletin No. 8 (if not available at your county extension office), *Home Canning of Fruits and Vegetables.* Write to: Government Printing Office, Publication Service Station, STOP SSOS, Washington, D.C. 20240 for price and ordering information.

2. Assemble all utensils: Pressure canner, Mason jars, lids, bands, tongs or jar lifter, timer, cooling racks, wide-mouth funnel, slotted spoon, wooden or plastic spatula, colander.

Use only Mason jars for home canning. These self-sealing, airtight jars are safe for canning because the glass is heat-tempered, which is especially important for pressure canning.

3. *Examine and clean all equipment.* Check all bands for rust, dents, or nicks and jars for chips and cracks.

Wash all equipment in hot, soapy water, but do not immerse top of pressure canner in water—just wipe it with a clean, damp cloth.

Keep clean jars and screw tops hot. Follow the manufacturer's instructions for preparation of the lids.

4. *Prepare freshest, cleanest greens possible.* Use freshly picked, tender greens and remove stems and imperfect leaves. Wash greens thoroughly in several changes of water, lifting the greens out and letting the grit settle to the bottom.

5. *Greens must be processed hot-pack (precooked).* Steam (in just enough water to prevent sticking, or use steamer) about 2½ pounds of greens three to five minutes, or until thoroughly wilted. To hasten wilting and prevent overcooking, turn greens over when steam begins to rise around edges of pan. Cut through greens with sharp knife, then pack the greens in hot jars, leaving about 1 inch headspace.

If desired for flavor, add salt, ½ teaspoon per pint or 1 teaspoon per quart. Cover with boiling water, retaining 1 inch headspace. Remove air bubbles by running nonmetallic spatula around inside jar. Adjust jar lids.

6. *Process in pressure canner.* Pack only the number of jars your pressure canner can accommodate at one time. Put the canner on the burner, and put the jars on the rack in the canner. Add 2 inches of boiling water to the canner. Allow enough space between the jars and the

sides of the pot so that the steam can flow freely. Clamp the lid securely.

Leave the valve or petcock open, and set the canner over high heat until steam has escaped for ten minutes. Then close the petcock or put on the weighted gauge, and let the pressure rise to 10 pounds. Start timing and keep adjusting the heat so that the pressure remains constant. If the pressure drops below 10 pounds, the processing time must be started again.

Processing Time

Altitude affects pressure canners. You may need to use more pressure at higher altitudes.

Feet Above Sea Level	Pressure	Processing Time
0–2000 feet	10 lbs	Pints: 70 minutes Quarts: 90 minutes
2000–3000 feet	11.5 lbs	Pints: 70 minutes Quarts: 90 minutes

If using a weight control canner, increase pressure to 15 pounds at elevations higher than 2,000 feet.

Do not skimp on processing time!

7. *After processing time is completed, turn off heat and wait until pressure has dropped to zero before opening canner.* Using tongs or jar lifter, remove the jars and place them upright on a rack or thick towel in a draft-free area, allowing enough room between jars so air may circulate freely. Do not tighten the screw bands on the dome lids; you may break the seals.

8. Check the seals after 24 hours.

(a) As the vacuum forms, the lid pulls down into the jar and makes a kerplunking sound.

(b) After cooling, the lid will be dished in the middle and should stay that way as long as the vacuum is present. You can feel it.

(c) After cooling, press the top of the lid with your thumb. If it makes a clicking sound, the seal is not complete.

If you find some jars with incomplete seals, put the jars in the refrigerator, and use the food soon. The greens are perfectly good to eat. They just won't hold in storage with imperfect seals.

9. Wipe the jars with a clean, damp cloth and remove the screw bands for reuse. Label the produce clearly, including the date. Store in a cool, dark, dry area.

10. Before serving, reheat all greens by boiling them in an open kettle for fifteen minutes. If they smell "off," or if the color or appearance doesn't look right, just dispose of them carefully.

FREEZING GREENS

Frozen greens can often be substituted with success in recipes calling for fresh-cooked greens. They aren't quite as good, but they sure are better than nothing.

Since about 2 pounds of greens reduce to 10 ounces when wilted, it's easy to realize that you'll need a whole "mess o' greens" in order to have some to freeze plus enough to eat fresh. So if you like greens, just know that it's difficult to plant too much.

For best freezing results, follow these simple steps:

1. *Select young, tender leaves.* Remove tough stems and imperfect leaves. You may chop them into smaller pieces if you wish.

2. *Wash greens thoroughly* in several changes of water. Swish them around in a basin of water, and lift them out to drain. The grit will sink to the bottom.

3. *Blanch greens in a kettle of boiling water.* Almost all greens (beet, chard, kale, mustard, New Zealand, and regular spinach and turnip) require two minutes' blanching. The one exception is collards, and they should be blanched for three minutes. If the leaves are very tender, blanch for only one and a half minutes.

4. *Chill greens immediately* in ice water to stop cooking process and to retain color. Chill for the same amount of time as they were cooked. Don't let them sit around in the water because they will lose flavor.

5. *Drain greens well* and pack in containers, leaving ½ inch headspace. Seal, label with contents, and date and freeze.

About the
National Gardening Association

The National Gardening Association is a nonprofit member-supported organization dedicated to helping people be successful gardeners at home, in community groups, and in institutions. We believe gardening adds joy and health to living, while improving the environment and encouraging an appreciation for the proper stewardship of the earth.

Established in 1972, this national organization of 250,000 members is now the premier membership organization for gardeners.

Members receive the monthly *National Gardening* magazine, may write the staff horticulturist for help with any gardening problem, receive discounts on gardening books, and get other member benefits. *National Gardening* magazine provides in-depth, how-to articles, profiles of members and their gardens, and evaluations of garden tools and products. Regional articles help members with special climate challenges. The magazine also provides a forum for NGA members in a "Seed Swap" exchange column, and seed and recipe search columns.

The National Gardening Association is a nationwide resource for information, services, and publications related to gardening. Besides the monthly magazine, NGA produces numerous books and directories for the home gardener. NGA also produces the annual *National Gardening Survey*, from research conducted for NGA by the Gallup Organization. This comprehensive report on trends in home gardening in America is widely used by the lawn and garden industry and is cited by the nation's media.

Well known as the information clearinghouse for community garden programs across the country, NGA offers on-site planning assistance, specialized manuals, a network to other organizations, and the annual National Gardening Grant Program—for gardens in neighborhoods, schools, and institutions, especially garden groups for youth, senior citizens, and people with disabilities.

The National Gardening Association continues to explore new ways to gather and share information, to connect gardeners with other gardeners, and to further its mission—successful gardeners everywhere!

If you would like a free sample issue of the *National Gardening* magazine and information on member benefits and how to join the National Gardening Association, please write or call:

The National Gardening Association
180 Flynn Avenue
Burlington, Vermont 05401
(802) 863-1308

Villard's National Gardening Association Series

75000-4 ☐ **BOOK OF TOMATOES**	$4.95; in Canada, $7.50
74991-X ☐ **BOOK OF LETTUCE & GREENS**	$4.95; in Canada, $7.50
74990-1 ☐ **BOOK OF EGGPLANT, OKRA & PEPPERS**	$4.95; in Canada, $7.50
74988-X ☐ **BOOK OF CUCUMBERS, MELONS &** **SQUASH**	$4.95; in Canada, $7.50

To order, send check or money order (no cash or CODs) to:

Villard Books, c/o Random House, Inc., 400 Hahn Road, Westminster, MD 21157

Please enclose $1.00 for the first book and 50¢ for each additional book to cover postage and handling. Make checks payable to Villard Books. If you have a major credit card, you can charge by phone by calling:

(800) 638-6460

You may also charge to your credit card by mailing in this coupon.

Please send me the books I have checked above.

NAME (please print)

ADDRESS

CITY/STATE   ZIP

PLEASE CHECK ONE: MASTERCARD ☐   VISA ☐
                                        AMERICAN EXPRESS ☐

CARD NUMBER

EXPIRATION DATE

SIGNATURE

Please add applicable sales tax. Allow 4–6 weeks for delivery.